"Money Mastery: The Ultimate Guide to Financial Independence"

I0490539

Preface:

Financial independence is a dream for many people, but it can seem like an unattainable goal. With so many financial decisions to make, from budgeting and saving to investing and protecting your assets, it can be overwhelming to know where to start. That's why I've written this book, "Money Mastery: The Ultimate Guide to Financial Independence."

In this book, I aim to provide you with a comprehensive guide to achieving financial independence. Whether you're just starting on your financial journey or looking to take your financial knowledge to the next level, this book has something for you. I've included practical advice, strategies, and tools that you can use to build your financial future and achieve your goals.

Each chapter of this book covers a different aspect of financial independence, from understanding money and creating a budget to building wealth and making smart financial decisions. I've included real-world examples and statistics to help illustrate key points and make the information more accessible.

Throughout this book, my focus is on providing you with actionable steps that you can take to improve your financial situation. I believe that financial independence is within reach for anyone who is willing to put in the time, effort, and dedication to make it happen.

So if you're ready to take control of your financial future, dive into the pages of "Money Mastery: The Ultimate Guide to Financial Independence" and start your journey towards financial freedom.

Introduction:

Welcome to "Money Mastery: The Ultimate Guide to Financial Independence," where you will discover the keys to achieving financial freedom and the power to control your financial future.

Do you find yourself struggling to make ends meet or living paycheck to paycheck? Or maybe you have a desire to retire early and live a life free from financial worries? Whatever your goals may be, financial independence is crucial to achieving them.

Financial independence means having enough wealth to support your lifestyle without having to rely on a job or a traditional source of income. It gives you the freedom to pursue your passions, take risks, and enjoy life on your own terms. But how can you attain financial independence?

The answer lies in having a plan. A well-crafted financial plan is essential for achieving your financial goals, whether that be paying off debt, saving for a down payment on a house, or building a retirement nest egg. A plan helps you track your progress, stay motivated, and make informed decisions about your money.

In this book, we will explore the fundamentals of money management and provide you with practical advice on how to create a plan that works for you. We will cover topics such as budgeting, saving and investing, managing debt, building wealth, protecting your assets, and making smart financial decisions.

According to a recent survey, 78% of Americans are living paycheck to paycheck, with little or no savings to fall back on in case of an emergency. We want to change that statistic and help you take control of your financial life. By following the steps outlined in this book, you can achieve financial independence and live the life you've always dreamed of.

So, if you're ready to take the first step towards financial freedom, let's dive in and discover the secrets of money mastery.

Chapter 1: Understanding Money

Money is a fundamental aspect of our daily lives. We use it to buy goods and services, pay bills, save for the future, and invest in opportunities that can generate wealth. However, managing money effectively can be challenging, especially if you don't have a solid understanding of the basics of money management, common financial terms and concepts, and the impact of inflation and interest rates.

In this chapter, we will explore these topics in detail, providing you with the knowledge you need to make informed financial decisions and take control of your financial future.

The Basics of Money Management

Managing your money effectively starts with understanding your income, expenses, and spending habits. A budget is an essential tool for achieving this goal. It allows you to track your income and expenses, identify areas where you can cut back, and prioritize your spending based on your goals and values.

Creating a budget requires you to determine your net income, which is your income after taxes and other deductions. Next, you need to identify your fixed expenses, such as rent, utilities, and insurance, as well as your variable expenses, such as food, entertainment, and clothing.

Once you have a clear understanding of your income and expenses, you can create a plan for how you will allocate your money each month. This plan should include saving for emergencies and long-term goals, such as retirement or a down payment on a house.

Common Financial Terms and Concepts

To make informed financial decisions, you need to have a solid understanding of common financial terms and concepts. Here are some key terms and concepts to know:

- Asset: Any item of value that you own which value will not depreciate over time, or investment.

- Liability: Any debt or obligation that you owe, such as a mortgage, credit card debt, or student loans.

- Net worth: The difference between your assets and liabilities.

- Interest: The amount of money you pay for the use of borrowed money.

- Inflation: The rate at which the general level of prices for goods and services is rising.

- Compound interest: Interest that is calculated not only on the initial principal but also on the accumulated interest from previous periods.

- Diversification: The practice of spreading your investments across different asset classes to reduce risk.

Understanding these terms and concepts can help you make informed decisions about your finances and investments.

The Impact of Inflation and Interest Rates

Inflation and interest rates are two critical factors that affect your finances. Inflation refers to the increase in the cost of goods and services over time. Interest rates, on the other hand, refer to the cost of borrowing money or the return on investments.

When inflation is high, the cost of goods and services goes up, which can reduce your purchasing power. For example, if the inflation rate is 3%, you will need $103 next year to buy what you can buy for $100 today.

Interest rates also play a crucial role in your financial life. High-interest rates can make it more expensive to borrow money, while low-interest rates can make it easier and more affordable to borrow money. Interest rates can also impact your investments. For example, when interest rates are low, bond yields tend to be lower, which can reduce the return on your investments.

Understanding inflation and interest rates is essential for making informed financial decisions. By staying informed about these factors, you can make strategic decisions about your investments and borrowing.

Conclusion

In conclusion, understanding money management, common financial terms and concepts, and the impact of inflation and interest rates is essential for achieving financial success. By creating a budget, understanding key financial terms and concepts, and staying informed about inflation and interest rates, you can make informed decisions about your finances and investments, take control of your financial future, and achieve your financial goals.

Chapter 2: Creating a Budget

A budget is a plan that helps you manage your money effectively. It is a tool that enables you to track your income and expenses, and identify areas where you can save or cut costs. A budget can help you achieve your financial goals, such as saving for a down payment on a house, paying off debt, or building an emergency fund.

Why a Budget is Important

Creating and sticking to a budget is essential for several reasons. Here are a few reasons why a budget is important:

1. Helps you manage your money: A budget helps you keep track of your income and expenses, so you know exactly where your money is going. It also helps you identify areas where you can cut costs and save money.

2. Helps you achieve your financial goals: A budget helps you prioritize your spending, so you can allocate your money towards your financial goals. Whether it's saving for a down payment on a house or paying off debt, a budget can help you stay on track and achieve your goals.

3. Helps you avoid overspending: A budget helps you avoid overspending by setting limits on your spending. This can prevent you from accumulating debt and falling into financial trouble.

Steps to Create a Budget

Creating a budget may seem overwhelming at first, but it's actually a straightforward process. Here are the steps to create a budget:

Step 1: Calculate Your Income

The first step in creating a budget is to calculate your income. This includes any money you earn from your job, investments, or other sources. Make sure to include all sources of income and calculate your total monthly income.

Step 2: Track Your Expenses

The next step is to track your expenses. This includes all your monthly expenses, such as rent, utilities, groceries, transportation, and entertainment. Make sure to track all of your expenses, no matter how small they may be. You can use a budgeting app or a spreadsheet to track your expenses.

Step 3: Categorize Your Expenses

Once you've tracked your expenses, you can categorize them into different groups, such as housing, transportation, food, and entertainment. This will help you identify areas where you're spending more money than you should be.

Step 4: Set Your Budget

The next step is to set your budget. Start by setting limits on your spending in each category. For example, you may decide to allocate $500 for groceries, $200 for transportation, and $100 for entertainment. Make sure to set realistic limits based on your income and expenses.

Step 5: Monitor Your Spending

After you've set your budget, it's important to monitor your spending to make sure you're sticking to your budget. You can do this by reviewing your expenses regularly and making adjustments as necessary. You may need to adjust your budget if you're consistently overspending in a particular category.

Tips for Sticking to a Budget

Creating a budget is one thing, but sticking to it is another. Here are some tips to help you stick to your budget:

1. Use a budgeting app: There are many budgeting apps available that can help you track your expenses and stay on top of your budget.

2. Avoid impulse purchases: Before making a purchase, ask yourself if it's something you really need. If it's not, consider waiting a few days before making the purchase.

3. Plan ahead: Plan your meals for the week ahead of time and make a grocery list. This can help you avoid overspending on food.

4.   Avoid credit card debt: If possible, avoid using credit cards to make purchases. If you do use a credit card, make sure to pay off the balance in full each month.

5.   Be flexible: Your budget is not set in stone. If you need to make adjustments, such as increasing your budget for a particular category, don't be afraid to do so. The key is to make sure you're still staying within your overall budget.

6.   Find ways to save: Look for ways to save money, such as by using coupons, buying in bulk, or shopping during sales. Small savings can add up over time and help you stay on track with your budget.

7.   Set realistic goals: When setting your budget, make sure to set realistic goals. If your goals are too ambitious, you may become discouraged and give up on your budget altogether.

8.   Review your budget regularly: Review your budget on a regular basis to make sure you're still on track. This can help you identify areas where you may need to make adjustments.

9.   Celebrate your successes: When you reach a financial goal, celebrate your success. This can help motivate you to continue working towards your other financial goals.

Conclusion

Creating a budget is an important step towards financial independence. It can help you manage your money effectively, achieve your financial goals, and avoid overspending. By following the steps outlined in this chapter and using the tips for sticking to a budget, you can take control of your finances and work towards a more secure financial future. Remember, creating a budget is just the first step - sticking to it is the key to success.

Chapter 3: Saving and Investing

Saving and investing are two critical elements in the pursuit of financial independence. Saving enables you to establish a financial cushion and offers a way to weather unexpected expenses or periods of unemployment. Investing, on the other hand, provides a means to grow your wealth over time, potentially achieving your long-term financial goals such as purchasing a home, paying for education, or planning for retirement. This chapter will discuss the importance of saving, the various types of savings accounts, the different investment options available, and how to develop an effective investment strategy.

The Importance of Saving

Saving is a vital component of achieving financial independence. It provides a foundation of financial security and stability, enabling you to handle any financial emergency or hardship that may arise. Saving helps to build your wealth, ensuring that you have enough money to meet your financial needs, now and in the future. It also enables you to make the most of investment opportunities when they present themselves.

Different Types of Savings Accounts

Various types of savings accounts are available, each with their advantages and disadvantages. The following are some common types of savings accounts:

1. Traditional Savings Accounts: These are standard savings accounts offered by banks and credit unions. They offer easy access to your funds, and you can deposit and withdraw money as often as you like. The interest rates on these accounts are usually low, but they remain a popular choice for many people.

2. Money Market Accounts: Money market accounts are similar to traditional savings accounts, but they offer higher interest rates. They also come with higher minimum balance requirements, and you may have to limit the number of withdrawals you make each month.

3. Certificates of Deposit (CDs): CDs are a type of savings account that offers a fixed interest rate for a specified period, typically ranging from six months to five years. They require a minimum deposit and a specific term, and if you withdraw your funds before the maturity date, you may incur a penalty.

Understanding Investment Options

Investing enables you to grow your wealth over time, but it comes with risks. It is essential to understand the different types of investment options available to you before committing your funds. Here are some common investment options:

1. Stocks: Stocks are a type of investment that represents ownership in a company. When you buy a stock, you become a shareholder in that company, and your investment may increase or decrease in value over time. Stocks offer the potential for high returns, but they also come with high risks.

2. Bonds: Bonds are debt securities issued by corporations or governments. When you buy a bond, you lend money to the issuer, who pays you interest until the bond matures. Bonds are generally considered less risky than stocks, but they offer lower returns.

3. Mutual Funds: Mutual funds are investment vehicles that pool money from multiple investors to buy a diversified portfolio of stocks, bonds, or other securities. They offer diversification and professional management, but they also come with fees and expenses.

Developing an Investment Strategy

An investment strategy helps you to achieve your financial goals, manage risk, and maximize returns. Here are some steps to develop a sound investment strategy:

1. Set Your Financial Goals: Determine what you want to achieve financially, such as buying a home, paying for education, or saving for retirement.

2. Determine Your Risk Tolerance: Assess your willingness to take on risk in exchange for potential returns. Your risk tolerance should consider your financial goals, investment timeline, and financial situation.

3. Diversify Your Portfolio: Diversification is key to managing risk in your investment portfolio. By investing in a variety of stocks, bonds, and other securities, you can reduce the impact of any one investment on your overall portfolio.

4. Monitor Your Portfolio: Regularly monitor your investment portfolio to ensure it remains aligned with your financial goals and risk tolerance.

5. Rebalance Your Portfolio: Over time, the performance of different investments in your portfolio will change, causing the allocation to shift. Rebalancing involves selling investments that have performed well and buying those that have performed poorly to maintain the target asset allocation.

6. Invest for the Long Term: Investing is a long-term process, and it is essential to avoid making decisions based on short-term market fluctuations. By investing for the long term, you can ride out market ups and downs and achieve your financial goals.

Conclusion

Saving and investing are vital components of achieving financial independence. Saving enables you to establish a financial cushion and provides a foundation of financial security and stability. Investing, on the other hand, provides a means to grow your wealth over time and achieve your long-term financial goals. By understanding the different types of savings accounts and investment options available and developing an effective investment strategy, you can maximize your returns while managing risk. Remember, investing is a long-term process, and it is essential to remain patient and disciplined in your approach.

Chapter 4: Managing Debt

Debt is an important financial issue that can significantly impact your financial independence. Managing your debt effectively can help you reduce your financial stress and improve your financial situation. In this chapter, we will discuss the different types of debt, creating a debt repayment plan, strategies for paying off debt faster, and how to avoid getting into debt in the future.

Types of Debt

Debt comes in many different forms, and it is essential to understand the different types of debt before you can manage it effectively. Some of the most common types of debt include:

1. Credit Card Debt: Credit card debt is one of the most prevalent types of debt in the US. Credit cards come with high-interest rates, making it easy to accumulate debt quickly.

2. Student Loans: Student loans are a type of debt used to finance higher education. While they are generally lower interest rates than credit card debt, they can still be a significant financial burden for graduates.

3. Mortgage Debt: Mortgage debt is the debt incurred when buying a home. It is generally considered "good" debt as it allows individuals to invest in a valuable asset that appreciates over time.

4. Auto Loans: Auto loans are used to finance the purchase of a car. Like credit card debt, auto loans come with high-interest rates, and the value of the car depreciates over time.

Creating a Debt Repayment Plan

Once you understand the types of debt you have, the next step is to create a debt repayment plan. A debt repayment plan involves prioritizing your debts and paying them off systematically.

1. Prioritize Your Debts: Start by listing all of your debts, including the balance, interest rate, and monthly payment. Prioritize your debts based on interest rate and focus on paying off high-interest debt first.

2. Set a Budget: Create a budget to help you allocate your money towards debt repayment. Identify areas where you can cut back on spending to free up more money for debt repayment.

3. Make Extra Payments: Make extra payments towards your debt whenever possible. Even small additional payments can make a big difference over time.

4. Consider Debt Consolidation: Debt consolidation involves combining multiple debts into a single loan with a lower interest rate. This can help simplify your debt repayment and reduce your overall interest payments.

Strategies for Paying Off Debt Faster

In addition to creating a debt repayment plan, there are several strategies you can use to pay off debt faster.

1. Snowball Method: The snowball method involves focusing on paying off the smallest debt first while making minimum payments on larger debts. Once the smallest debt is paid off, move on to the next smallest debt, and so on.

2. Avalanche Method: The avalanche method involves prioritizing debts based on interest rate and focusing on paying off high-interest debt first.

3. Balance Transfer: A balance transfer involves moving high-interest credit card debt to a card with a lower interest rate, allowing you to save on interest payments and pay off the debt faster.

How to Avoid Getting into Debt in the Future

While paying off your current debt is important, it is also essential to avoid getting into debt in the future. Here are some tips to help you avoid getting into debt:

1. Create a Budget: Creating a budget can help you manage your money effectively and avoid overspending.

2. Build an Emergency Fund: An emergency fund can help you avoid using credit cards or other forms of debt in the event of an unexpected expense.

3. Use Credit Cards Responsibly: Use credit cards responsibly, paying off the balance in full each month to avoid accumulating debt.

4. Avoid Lifestyle Inflation: As your income increases, it can be tempting to increase your spending. Avoid lifestyle inflation by keeping your spending in check and saving more of your income.

Additionally, if you're struggling with debt repayment, consider reaching out to a financial advisor or credit counseling service. These professionals can help you develop a personalized plan for getting out of debt and staying on track financially.

It's also important to note that avoiding debt altogether may not be realistic for everyone. For example, taking out a mortgage to buy a home may be necessary for many people. However, by being aware of the types of debt you're taking on and having a plan for repayment, you can minimize the negative impact that debt can have on your financial situation.

Conclusion.

In summary, managing debt is a crucial component of achieving financial independence. By understanding the types of debt you have, creating a repayment plan, and avoiding taking on unnecessary debt, you can take control of your finances and work towards a more secure financial future.

Chapter 5: Building Wealth

Building wealth is a long-term process that involves smart decision-making and discipline. It's important to understand that there is no one-size-fits-all solution to building wealth, as everyone's financial situation and goals are unique. However, there are several ways to increase your chances of building wealth over time.

1.   Investing in the stock market

Investing in the stock market is one of the most popular ways to build wealth. Historically, the stock market has provided higher returns than other investment vehicles such as savings accounts or bonds. By investing in individual stocks, mutual funds, or exchange-traded funds (ETFs), you can potentially earn high returns over time.

For example, if you had invested $10,000 in the S&P 500 index in 1980 and left it untouched, it would have grown to nearly $600,000 by the end of 2020. However, it's important to note that investing in the stock market also comes with risks and it's important to do your research before making any investment decisions.

2.   Real estate investing

Investing in real estate is another popular way to build wealth. Real estate can provide passive income through rental properties and appreciation in property value over time. Additionally, real estate can be a hedge against inflation, as property values typically rise with inflation.

For example, if you had purchased a rental property for $100,000 in 1980 and rented it out for $1,000 per month, by 2020 the property could be worth $500,000 and you would have earned over $400,000 in rental income.

3.   Starting a business

Starting a business is another way to build wealth. Successful entrepreneurs can earn significant income and build wealth through their businesses. However, starting a business comes with risks and requires a significant amount of time, effort, and capital.

For example, Jeff Bezos, the founder of Amazon, started the company in his garage in 1994 and is now worth over $170 billion. While not everyone will achieve this level of success, starting a business can be a rewarding way to build wealth.

4. Maximize your earning potential

Maximizing your earning potential is another important aspect of building wealth. This can include increasing your education or skills to qualify for higher-paying jobs, negotiating a higher salary or benefits, or starting a side business or freelancing gig to supplement your income.

For example, if you earned an additional $10,000 per year for 30 years by negotiating higher salaries or starting a side business, you would have earned an additional $300,000 over that time period.

5.   Live below your means

Living below your means is a fundamental aspect of building wealth. This means spending less than you earn and avoiding unnecessary expenses. By living below your means, you can save money and invest in your future.

For example, if you saved $500 per month and invested it in the stock market for 30 years, with an average annual return of 8%, you would have over $500,000 by the end of that time period.

6.   Develop a retirement plan

Developing a retirement plan is crucial for building long-term wealth. This can include contributing to a 401(k) or IRA, investing in real estate or other income-producing assets, or creating a diversified investment portfolio.

For example, if you contributed $500 per month to a 401(k) for 30 years and earned an average annual return of 8%, you would have over $750,000 in your retirement account by the end of that time period.

Overall, building wealth takes time, effort, and discipline. By combining these various approaches to building wealth and being diligent about managing your finances, you can achieve long-term financial independence and security.

Chapter 6: Protecting Your Assets

As you work towards financial independence, it is important to protect the assets you have already accumulated. Unexpected events such as accidents, illness, or natural disasters can easily wipe out years of hard work and savings if you are not properly insured. In this chapter, we will discuss the importance of insurance, the different types of insurance, and how to choose the right insurance for your needs.

Understanding Insurance

Insurance is a financial product that helps you protect against financial loss from unexpected events. You pay a premium to an insurance company, and in exchange, they agree to cover the costs of certain events, such as a car accident or a house fire. Insurance allows you to transfer the risk of financial loss to an insurance company, giving you peace of mind that you will not be financially devastated by an unexpected event.

Types of Insurance

There are many types of insurance, and it can be overwhelming to determine which types you need. Here are some common types of insurance to consider:

1.   Auto Insurance: Auto insurance is required by law in most states and covers the costs of damage to your vehicle or another person's vehicle if you are at fault in an accident.

2.	Homeowners or Renters Insurance: Homeowners insurance covers the costs of damage to your home and personal property due to events like fire, theft, or natural disasters. Renters insurance covers the cost of damage to your personal property and provides liability protection if someone is injured in your rental unit.

3.	Health Insurance: Health insurance covers the costs of medical care, including doctor visits, hospitalization, and prescription drugs.

4.	Life Insurance: Life insurance provides financial protection for your loved ones in the event of your death. There are different types of life insurance policies, including term life insurance and whole life insurance.

5.	Disability Insurance: Disability insurance provides income replacement if you become unable to work due to a disability.

Choosing the Right Insurance

Choosing the right insurance for your needs can be challenging. Here are some tips to help you make the best decision:

1.	Assess your risks: Think about the risks you face and the potential financial impact of those risks. This will help you determine which types of insurance you need.

2.	Shop around: Get quotes from multiple insurance companies to find the best coverage and price.

3.	Consider deductibles: A higher deductible means you pay more out of pocket if an event occurs, but your premiums will be lower.

4.	Understand the policy: Read the policy carefully to understand what is covered and what is not. Ask questions if you are unclear about anything.

5.   Work with an agent: An insurance agent can help you understand your options and find the right coverage for your needs.

Conclusion

Insurance is an important part of protecting your assets and achieving financial independence. By understanding the different types of insurance and choosing the right coverage for your needs, you can have peace of mind that you are protected from unexpected financial losses. Remember to assess your risks, shop around, consider deductibles, understand the policy, and work with an agent to make the best decision for your financial future.

Chapter 7: Building a Financial Support System

Achieving financial independence is not an easy task, and it often requires a support system to help you along the way. A support system can provide guidance, advice, and motivation to help you stay on track and achieve your financial goals. In this chapter, we will discuss the importance of a financial support system, how to find financial advisors and professionals, and how to develop a network of mentors and peers.

The Importance of a Support System

Having a support system in place can make all the difference when it comes to achieving financial independence. It can provide you with a sounding board to bounce ideas off of, and a group of people who share your goals and can help you stay motivated.

Studies have shown that having a support system can also have a significant impact on your financial success. According to a study by Fidelity Investments, people who work with financial advisors are more likely to save more money, have a better understanding of their investments, and feel more confident about their financial future than those who do not work with an advisor.

Finding Financial Advisors and Professionals

Finding the right financial advisor or professional can be a daunting task, but it is a crucial step in building a financial support system. The first step is to identify your needs and what you are looking for in an advisor. Are you looking for someone to help you with investment management, retirement planning, or debt reduction?

Once you have identified your needs, you can begin your search for a financial advisor or professional. There are many resources available to help you find a reputable advisor, including online directories, referrals from friends and family, and professional organizations like the National Association of Personal Financial Advisors (NAPFA) or the Financial Planning Association (FPA).

When choosing a financial advisor, it is important to do your due diligence and ask the right questions. Some important factors to consider include their experience, credentials, and investment philosophy. It is also important to ensure that they are a fiduciary, which means that they are legally obligated to act in your best interests.

Developing a Network of Mentors and Peers

In addition to working with a financial advisor or professional, it can be helpful to develop a network of mentors and peers who can provide additional support and guidance. These may be people in your personal or professional network who have experience with financial planning, investing, or entrepreneurship.

Networking events and industry conferences can be great places to meet new people and expand your network. Additionally, there are many online communities and forums where you can connect with like-minded individuals and seek advice on a variety of financial topics.

Mentors can also be a valuable resource in helping you navigate your career and financial journey. A mentor is someone who has experience and expertise in a particular area and can provide guidance and advice based on their own experiences. Mentors can help you set goals, develop a plan, and hold you accountable for your progress.

Conclusion

Building a financial support system is an important step in achieving financial independence. Whether you work with a financial advisor, develop a network of mentors and peers, or both, having a support system in place can help you stay on track and achieve your goals. By utilizing the resources available to you, you can build a strong foundation for your financial future.

Chapter 8: Making Smart Financial Decisions

In the pursuit of financial independence, making smart financial decisions is crucial. This chapter will provide strategies for making wise choices, avoiding common financial pitfalls, and emphasizing the importance of staying informed and educated.

Strategies for making wise financial choices:

1.   Set financial goals: Setting clear and achievable financial goals is an essential first step towards making smart financial decisions. Goals should be specific, measurable, achievable, relevant, and time-bound. By setting goals, you can prioritize your spending and focus on what's most important to you.

2.   Create a financial plan: A financial plan can help you map out a path towards achieving your financial goals. It should include a budget, a savings plan, and an investment strategy. A financial plan can also help you prepare for emergencies and unexpected expenses.

3.   Do your research: Before making any significant financial decision, do your research. This may involve comparing different products or services, reading reviews, and consulting with professionals. Make sure you understand the terms and conditions and any fees associated with your financial decisions.

4.   Avoid impulsive decisions: Making impulsive financial decisions can be detrimental to your financial well-being. It's essential to take the time to reflect on your options and seek advice from professionals or trusted friends or family members.

How to avoid common financial pitfalls:

1. Overspending: Overspending is one of the most common financial pitfalls. It's essential to distinguish between wants and needs and to create a budget that reflects your priorities and goals.

2. Credit card debt: High-interest credit card debt can quickly spiral out of control. It's important to pay off your credit card balances in full each month and to avoid using credit cards for purchases you can't afford.

3. Lack of emergency savings: Unexpected expenses, such as medical bills or car repairs, can quickly derail your financial plans. Having an emergency fund with three to six months of living expenses can provide a safety net and prevent you from going into debt.

The importance of staying informed and educated:

1. Keep up-to-date with financial news: Staying informed about current financial news and trends can help you make informed decisions. Read reputable financial news sources and follow financial experts on social media.

2. Attend financial workshops and seminars: Attending financial workshops and seminars can help you learn new skills and strategies for managing your finances. You may also have the opportunity to connect with other like-minded individuals and expand your network.

3. Seek professional advice: Consulting with a financial advisor or other professionals can provide valuable insights into your financial situation and help you make informed decisions. It's essential to find professionals who are reputable and have your best interests at heart.

In conclusion, making smart financial decisions is crucial to achieving financial independence. By setting clear financial goals, creating a financial plan, avoiding common financial pitfalls, and staying informed and educated, you can take control of your finances and work towards a brighter financial future.

Conclusion:

Throughout this book, we have discussed the essential components of achieving financial independence. From understanding the basics of money management in Chapter 1 to making smart financial decisions in Chapter 8, we have provided a comprehensive guide to building a solid financial foundation.

Chapter 1 taught us the importance of understanding money and the impact of inflation and interest rates. We also learned the common financial terms and concepts that are crucial for effective money management. By grasping these concepts, we can create a strong foundation for finances.

In Chapter 2, we explored the importance of creating a budget and the steps involved in making one. We also provided tips for sticking to a budget and achieving financial goals. By understanding the value of budgeting and the methods to create a budget, we can stay on top of our expenses and reach our financial objectives.

Chapter 3 delved into the critical aspect of saving and investing. We learned about the different types of savings accounts, investment options, and developing an investment strategy. By mastering these concepts, we can maximize our earning potential and secure our financial future.

In Chapter 4, we examined how to manage debt effectively. We covered the types of debt, creating a debt repayment plan, strategies for paying off debt faster, and how to avoid getting into debt in the future. By implementing these strategies, we can reduce our debt and improve our credit score.

In Chapter 5, we explored various ways to build wealth, such as maximizing our earning potential, developing a retirement plan, and investing in real estate or stocks. By diversifying our investments and focusing on long-term wealth building strategies, we can create financial security for ourselves and our families.

Chapter 6 emphasized the importance of protecting our assets through insurance. We learned about the different types of insurance and how to choose the right one for our needs. By understanding the value of insurance and choosing the appropriate coverage, we can mitigate financial risks and protect our assets.

In Chapter 7, we discussed building a financial support system, which includes finding financial advisors and professionals, as well as developing a network of mentors and peers. By building a strong support system, we can gain valuable insights and advice to make informed financial decisions.

Finally, in Chapter 8, we explored strategies for making smart financial decisions and avoiding common financial pitfalls. By staying informed and educated about personal finance, we can make wise choices that align with our financial goals.

In conclusion, financial independence is achievable through proper money management, investing, and protecting our assets. By implementing the strategies outlined in this book and developing a solid financial plan, we can achieve financial freedom and live the life we desire. Remember that financial independence is a journey, not a destination, and with dedication and persistence, we can reach our financial goals.

www.ingramcontent.com/pod-product-compliance
Lightning Source LLC
Chambersburg PA
CBHW070758220526
45467CB00014B/782